EGG

C O O K B O O K

Marion Maxwell

ILLUSTRATED BY JUDITH O'DWYER

HarperCollins*Publishers*

First published in 1993 by
The Appletree Press Ltd

THE EGG COOKBOOK

HarperCollins books may be purchased for
educational, business, or sales promotional use.
For information please write: Special Markets
Department, HarperCollins Publishers, Inc., 10 East
53rd Street, New York, NY 10022.

FIRST EDITION

LIBRARY OF CONGRESS CATALOG CARD NUMBER:

92-52579

ISBN 0-06-016904-4

93 94 95 96 97 10 9 8 7 6 5 4 3 2 1

Introduction

In some other book I may attempt the definitive culinary history of the egg. It will tell at great length how primitive man collected birds' eggs and cooked them in ashes, how the Romans were first to domesticate hens on any scale and how they revered the egg for its aphrodisiac properties, how the Chinese recognized in it the perfect embodiment of yin and yang, how in the Middle Ages eggs were eaten on their sides, yes, and custards were eaten out of "coffins", how Queen Victoria was pleased once to eat an ostrich egg omelette, how writers' and opera singers' names have been immortalized (and politicians' reputations ruined) by association with the egg, not to mention what hen holds the record for laying, how spare egg whites can be used to plug a leaking car radiator, and who knows what other unconsidered trifles. Instead, I offer a little collection of recipes which I hope will represent to you the main culinary functions as well as some of the gastronomic delights of this most versatile, not to say indispensable, foodstuff. For some recipes you will need to use your judgement as to how many eggs people will want to eat. Remember – *un oeuf* can be as good as a feast!

Scrambling Graciously

There was a time when sniffy head waiters in grand hotels claimed to know a gentleman by the size of the breakfast he ordered. Today, when most of us struggle to work on little more than a bowl of cereal, luxury is a leisurely-cooked breakfast. Here are three suggestions for a gracious start to the day, all based on creamy scrambled eggs.

Beat 2–3 eggs well. Season with salt and white pepper. Melt generous tablespoon butter in a heavy saucepan, over a low heat. Add eggs and stir vigorously with a wooden spoon until starting to thicken. Add another pat of butter (some people also advocate an extra yolk or tablespoon cream) and remove from heat, stirring until eggs are evenly creamy. Serve at once. (Serves 1)

Mother's Day Brunch
Appreciative offspring acquire a fresh croissant, pile in scrambled egg, top with crisp slice of bacon and serve with love. (Serves 1)

Millionaire's Eggs
Pile creamy scrambled eggs into shells that have been carefully emptied by removing a "lid". Set in beautiful egg-cups, top with caviar and fantasize. (Serves 1)

Smoked Salmon Parcels
Prepare ahead and breakfast in bed! Add some snipped chives and smoked salmon trimmings to scrambled eggs. Make rectangles of thinly-sliced smoked salmon and wrap spoonfuls of mixture to make small parcels. Tie prettily with chives. Eat cool, or brush with melted butter and reheat gently over steam. (Serves 1)

Eggs Benedict

This classic brunch dish, once a speciality of the Algonquin Hotel in New York, features poached eggs topped with one of the classic sauces that depend on the emulsifying properties of eggs. Dispense with double boilers and worries about curdling and make your hollandaise sauce by the blender method.

3 muffins, split, toasted and buttered
6 rounds cooked ham
6 very fresh eggs, lightly poached
salt and white pepper
Hollandaise sauce:
3 egg yolks
1 tbsp mixed lemon juice and cold water
salt and pepper
$^1/_2$ lb melted butter
(Serves 4)

To make sauce, put yolks in blender with liquid and seasoning and blend for a few seconds. Melt butter gently until just beginning to froth and add to mixture in blender while running it at fairly high speed, to produce a thick cream. Keep warm.

Top hot buttered muffins with ham, then poached eggs and season. Spoon over sauce.

Eggs in Madeira Jelly

Set in sparkling, delicately flavored aspic, these eggs make a glamorous starter or a scene-stealer for a buffet table. They are traditionally set in little oval metal molds, then turned out to reveal a decoration set in the jelly. Improvise with tea-cups or simply make in ramekin dishes and decorate on top. Either way, here is an opportunity to make edible pictures!

4 oeufs mollets
scant cup aspic jelly
Madeira or port, to taste
4 small slices ham (optional)
Decoration:
tarragon leaves
chives, black olives
sliced carrot, red pepper etc.
(**Serves 4**)

Oeufs mollets are halfway between soft and hardboiled eggs. Boil for 5–6 minutes, and peel at once under cold running water.

For decorations cut carrot "flowers" from thin slices, cut black olives into long slices for "petals" or "leaves", use chives for stems etc. Heat aspic jelly and flavor to taste with port. Wet molds, set on a tray, then pour in aspic to a depth of $1/8$ inch. Make a picture decoration in the aspic, remembering that the eggs are to be turned out. Set tray in refrigerator until jelly sets. Place an egg in each mold and pour round enough aspic to fill mold clear of the egg. (The aspic should be nearly wet, but *just* still liquid – warm again gently, if necessary.) Arrange slice of ham, if using, around egg. When ready, quickly dip molds in hot water and turn out.

A Dip in the Mediterranean

Here are a trio of sauces-cum-dips, that contain ingredients characteristic of Mediterranean cuisine since Roman times.

Aïoli This "butter of Provence" is delicious with eggs, but it is also eaten with cold fish and crudités.

> 6 large cloves garlic   2 tbsp lemon juice
> 1 egg yolk   salt and pepper
> 1 cup good olive oil

Crush garlic with a little salt. Mix with egg yolk in medium bowl. Beat in the olive oil drop by drop until the mixture begins to thicken. Beat the mixture continuously – the oil can now be poured in a thin stream. When half the oil has been added, beat in the lemon juice and 2 teaspoons water. Whisk in remaining oil. Season.

Tapénade The ingredients which include capers or "tapéna" are characteristic of ancient Provençal peasant cooking.

> ½ cup anchovies   ½ cup tuna, drained
> ⅔ cup olive oil   4 cloves garlic
> ½ cup capers   2 cups black olives
> juice of 1 lemon   1–2 tbsp brandy
> mustard to taste   black pepper

Soak the anchovies in milk overnight to desalt them. Drain well. Pound all the ingredients together into a thick purée (you can do this in a blender). Gradually add the olive oil and lemon juice drop by drop, as for mayonnaise, to form a smooth paste. Add the mustard, brandy and black pepper to taste. Spread in a flat dish and top with halved hardboiled eggs or, as was traditionally done, add the egg yolks to the mixture and use to stuff the halves. Either way, serve with hot bread and toast.

The mixture is also eaten with a selection of lightly-cooked warm vegetables or with cold fish.

Skordaliá This is a Greek version of aïoli, but contains a favorite Greek ingredient, almonds.

> 6 cloves garlic   ¼ cup white breadcrumbs
> 2 egg yolks   lemon juice
> ½ cup olive oil   parsley
> 2 tbsp ground almonds

Pound the garlic in a mortar to a paste, then add yolks, followed by the olive oil, drop by drop as for mayonnaise. Stir in the ground almonds and the breadcrumbs. Loosen the sauce with plenty of lemon juice. Add chopped parsley.

East Meets West in a Pickle

Pickled Eggs The English pickled egg with the pint of beer has largely lost out to a package of potato chips. Here is how to recreate the tradition with a recipe that is superior to any commercial version. Hardboil 12 eggs. Boil up to 4½ cups of malt vinegar with 1 inch fresh ginger, 1 tablespoon coriander seeds and 2 tablespoons white peppercorns. Pack eggs into wide-mouthed jar, cover with hot vinegar and add 2 whole chillies. Seal. Use wine or cider vinegar for a milder version.

Marbled Tea Eggs These look decorative and have an exotic flavor. Try using a tea such as Broken Orange Pekoe. Serve if liked with a green mayonnaise. Hardboil 4 eggs. When cool, crack shells all over into a fine craze. In a small saucepan, bring to boil enough strong tea to cover eggs adding 2 tablespoons dark soy sauce, 1 tablespoon salt and ½ teaspoon aniseed. Simmer eggs for 1 hour. Cool in the liquid. Carefully shell eggs to reveal marbled effect. Best eaten straight away. To make a *sauce verte* blend some chopped fresh herbs with mayonnaise.

Poached Eggs Florentine

"Florentine" often refers to a garnish or bed of spinach in tribute to the Florentine chefs who first introduced the vegetable to France. Catherine de Medici brought her Italian cooks with her when she married King Henry II of France in 1533, thus also bringing about a fertile marriage of cuisines.

The sauce, the spinach, and the eggs can all be cooked ahead and assembled at the last minute. Add some triangles of toast and a slice of crispy bacon, or serve on a bed of rice for a lovely vegetarian meal.

2 cups spinach
1¼ cups cheese sauce
4 very fresh eggs
salt and pepper
1 tbsp butter

¼ cup Parmesan or
    cheddar cheese, grated
2–3 tbsp light cream
freshly grated nutmeg

(Serves 4)

Preheat oven to 375°F. Wash spinach well, put in pan with salt and just the water that clings, cook 10–15 minutes. Drain, mix with butter and season with salt, pepper, and nutmeg. Put in an oven-proof dish. Poach eggs lightly for approx. 3 minutes in about 11/2 inches barely simmering water, drain, and place side by side on the spinach. Spoon over cheese sauce, pour over cream, and sprinkle with grated cheese. Put dish in center of oven. Bake 10–15 minutes until golden. Brown under grill.

Eggs Mimosa

"I've met some hardboiled eggs in my time, but you're twenty minutes," said a character once in a Billy Wilder film. The sad culinary truth that lies behind the remark is that one of the worst travesties you can commit with an egg is to overcook a hardboiled one.

Nothing could be further from the concept of this dish for which the delicate blossom of the mimosa tree is the inspiration. It makes one of the simplest but most delicious ways to start a meal – nicely-judged hardboiled eggs, stuffed with prawns and finished with a coating of mayonnaise and a scattering of egg yolk "blossom".

8 hardboiled eggs
scant cup prawns
mayonnaise
watercress
Mayonnaise:
2 eggs yolks
1 tsp mustard

$1\frac{1}{8}$ cups good
quality oil (olive if liked)
1 tsp each white wine
vinegar and lemon juice
2 pinches salt and
white pepper

(Serves 4–6)

To make mayonnaise, whisk together egg yolks, mustard, salt and pepper. Add half the oil in a slow trickle, whisking steadily until mixture turns pale and thickens. Loosen with vinegar and lemon juice and whisk in remaining oil. Correct seasoning.

Split eggs in half lengthways, scoop out yolks and push half of them through a sieve into a basin. Add the prawns. Mix and bind with 1–2 tablespoons mayonnaise. Set whites on a serving dish. Fill with prawn mixture and sandwich together. Thin rest of mayonnaise slightly with 1 tablespoon hot water and coat the eggs with this. Hold sieve over eggs and push rest of yolks through. Garnish with watercress.

Quails' Eggs in Poppadom Nests
with a Curry Sabayon

Diminutive quails' eggs make an ideal subject for hors d'oeuvre or salads and give lots of scope for presentation. Eggs feature also in the sauce, a savory *sabayon*, much favored as an alternative to heavy cream sauces by exponents of *nouvelle cuisine*. For an exotic touch, garnish with flecks of gold *vark* (edible paper).

12 quails eggs
4 black pepper poppadoms
oil for deep frying
2 4-in metal sieves, preferably flat-bottomed
gold vark *(optional)*
Curry sabayon:
1 tsp curry powder and
1 tsp ghee or clarified
butter, gently cooked
together for five minutes
6 tbsp chicken stock
3 egg yolks
5 tbsp melted butter
pinch cayenne
lemon juice
4 tbsp heavy cream
(Serves 4)

Make the sauce up to half an hour in advance by whisking curry powder mixture with egg yolks and stock until it has tripled in volume. Stand bowl in hot water and continue whisking until sauce is smooth and like lightly whipped cream. Whisk in warm butter. Thin with a little more liquid if necessary. Season and add a little lemon juice to taste. Hardboil the eggs for two minutes and plunge into cold water.

To form the baskets: Soften poppadoms slightly in the steam of a kettle, then place between two sieves and plunge in hot oil for about 30 seconds, until crisp and golden. Drain on kitchen towel.

To assemble dish: Whisk the lightly-whipped cream into the *sabayon*. Spoon it into nests, set in eggs, and decorate.

Avgolémono

Should an egg appear in the soup course, it is sometimes in the form of a poached egg dropped in for extra substance. Here, however, in this best known of Greek soups, eggs and lemon juice liaise to thicken a chicken broth. In Cyprus it is eaten on Easter morning to break the long Lenten fast.

> *4 cups well-flavored home-made chicken stock*
> *¹/₄ cup white rice or small pasta*
> *2 eggs*
> *juice of 1 large or 2 small lemons*
> *salt and freshly ground black pepper*
> *1 tbsp freshly chopped parsley*
> **(Serves 4–6)**

Bring stock to the boil and add rice or pasta. Return to the boil and simmer 10–12 minutes until rice or pasta is tender. Beat eggs and add lemon juice. Remove stock from the heat and gradually add a ladleful to the egg mixture, stirring all the time. Add the rest of the broth, returning to a very low heat for a few minutes. Season to taste and add the parsley. Serve.

Eggs En Cocotte with Lettuce and Bacon

An egg, a dish, a little butter, a swirl of cream are all that is required for the basic version of this little classic egg dish but the possible additions to the feast are endless: herbs, cheese, mushrooms, truffles, salmon ... Here, lightly-sautéed lettuce and crispy bacon add an unexpected crunch which complements the lightly-baked egg. (Omit bacon if you prefer.) Cook either in the oven or over a hotplate.

approx. 2 tbsp cos lettuce (cut in strips)
pat of butter
1 rasher bacon, grilled until crisp
salt and black pepper
1 egg
2 tbsp cream
heaped tsp grated Parmesan cheese
a little extra butter
(Serves 1)

Preheat oven to 375°F. Sauté strips of crisp lettuce in a little butter for a few minutes over a low heat. Generously butter ramekin or "cocotte" dish, and preheat gently. Add lettuce and pieces of bacon. Season lightly. Break the egg on top. Combine cream and cheese and pour over egg. Cover dish with a plate or foil and set in shallow pan of water, either on top of the cooker or on a baking sheet in the oven. Bake for 4–8 minutes, depending on type and size of dish.

Oeufs À La Tripe

A tried and true egg'n'onion lunch or supper dish, great for those who can't eat cheese and a really tasty way to use up hardboiled eggs. It's delicious piled into a big baked potato or eaten with crusty bread and salad.

2 large Spanish onions
3 tbsp butter
2 tbsp flour
1 cup milk
nutmeg
salt and pepper
6 hardboiled eggs, peeled
2–3 tbsp heavy cream
fresh breadcrumbs
a little extra butter
(Serves 4)

Skin onions and slice thinly. Soften gently in butter until creamy. Shake in flour, add milk and stir to make a smooth sauce. Cook out slowly for 15 minutes and season. Slice eggs into gratin dish. Stir cream into sauce and pour over eggs. Sprinkle on crumbs and dot with butter. Heat through in the oven or under a gentle grill.

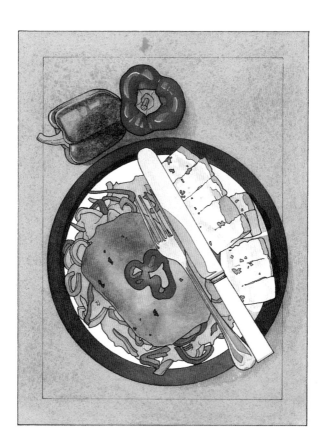

Pipérade

From the Basque country that straddles the French/Spanish border comes this rich stew of peppers, onions, and tomatoes into which eggs are scrambled at the last minute. The name derives from *piper*, Basque for "pepper". Traditionally the vegetables were sautéed in goose fat and the dish would be served with a slice of delicious *jambon de Bayonne*.

1 tbsp olive oil and either goose fat, bacon fat or butter
2 medium onions, thinly sliced
1 or 2 cloves garlic, crushed
4 small green or red peppers (or a mixture of both)
salt and freshly ground black pepper
1 lb tomatoes, skinned deseeded and chopped
1 tsp sugar
1/2 tsp dried basil (or a handful of fresh leaves, chopped)
4 large fresh eggs
(Serves 4)

Melt a pat of butter or fat and a tablespoon of olive oil in a shallow heavy pan and add the onions, cooking them very gently for 10 minutes without browning. Add the crushed garlic and peppers, stir everything around a little, season with salt and pepper, and cook without covering for about 15 minutes. Add tomatoes, a teaspoon of sugar, and the basil and cook gently until the tomatoes are almost in a pulp. Beat eggs thoroughly, pour them into the pan and, using a wooden spoon, stir as you would for scrambled eggs. As soon as mixture starts to thicken, remove pan from the heat, continuing to stir as the eggs gently set. Serve immediately topped with a slice of grilled gammon and hot garlic bread.

For a picnic, scoop out the center of a small French loaf, reserving lid. Spread inside and out with garlic butter and bake at 350°F until slightly crisp. Fill with *pipérade* and replace lid. Serve sliced when cold.

Green Vegetable Tart

Layers of vegetables are encased in cabbage leaves and set in a savory custard. Simplify the preparation by cooking the vegetables in advance.

head of green cabbage
5 leeks, weighing about 1 lb total
½ lb green beans
3 tbsp butter
1 clove garlic
1 cup sliced mushrooms
salt and pepper
Custard mixture:
2 eggs
2 egg yolks
⅔ cups milk
2 scant cups heavy cream
salt and pepper
pinch of ground nutmeg
(Serves 4)

Wash cabbage, remove large ribs, and boil 7–8 minutes or until tender. Drain, refresh under cold water, and dry well. Cut leeks until 1-inch lengths, and steam until barely tender. Refresh, and drain. Boil green beans until barely tender. Drain, refresh, and drain again. Purée with 1 tablespoon butter and crushed garlic. Sauté mushrooms in rest of butter and season. Set oven to 350°F. Mix up the custard ingredients. Butter a 9 inch diameter cake pan. Line bottom and sides with cabbage leaves, leaving some hanging over the edge to cover top of tart. Chop rest of cabbage. Season vegetables and layer then until all are used. Pour in custard mixture, fold over leaves, and bake for about 45–50 minutes until gently set.

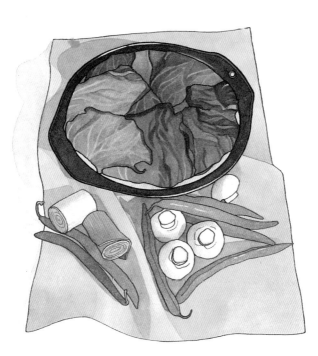

Seafood Pancakes

No eggs, no pancakes and how much poorer our cuisine would be. For these *crêpes aux fruits de mer* use any combination of seafood you may have, including prawns, scallops, sole, or smoked salmon. The filling is augmented by hardboiled eggs and bound in a tasty fish *velouté*. Stockpile the pancakes and assemble the whole dish in advance.

Seafood filling:	Pancake batter:
3 cups seafood (lightly cooked)	2 cups flour
3 chopped, hardboiled eggs	2 scant cups milk
$2/3$ cups each of fish stock and white wine	$2/3$ cups water
juice of 1 lemon	2 eggs and 1 extra yolk
6 tbsp butter	1 tsp curry powder
1 large onion, chopped	pinch salt
$1^1/2$ cups chopped mushrooms	1 tbsp oil
6 tbsp all-purpose flour	soda water
$1^1/3$ cups light cream	
chopped parsley	
$1/4$ cup grated cheese	

Preheat oven to 200°F. Whisk together all the pancake ingredients except the soda water. Leave batter to rest for $1/2$ hour. Add a good dash of soda water and make thin pancakes, stacking them between layers of kitchen towel. Sauté onion and mushrooms in butter until soft. Add flour, cook 1 minute and make into a sauce by adding stock, wine, lemon juice, and half the cream. Stir in parsley, add seasoning, and cool. Combine with seafood and use to fill pancakes, rolling them or folding them into parcels. Arrange in a greased ovenproof dish. Pour over rest of cream. Sprinkle with cheese and bake for 10–15 minutes.

The Perfect Omelette

Several restaurants in Mont St Michel, site of the spectacular citadel in Normandy, still honor the name of Mme. Poulard, whose *auberge* became famous in the early 1900s for the wonderful omelettes she turned out. Asked once for her secret by a Parisian chef, she replied: "I break some good eggs in a bowl, I beat them, I put a good piece of butter in the pan, I throw the eggs into it and I shake it constantly." Her modest reply may contain the hint that success lies not so much in the recipe as in a knack, and that knowing what not to do may also be significant. Speculation about the finer points of the classic French omelette continues, however. Add a little water? Omit one egg white? And reverence amounting almost to superstition has long surrounded the traditional cast-iron omelette pan, now largely removed by the advent of modern surfaces.

Some useful don'ts: Don't use too large a pan – 6-inch is perfect for two to three eggs. Don't beat eggs too much – stir with two forks. Don't cook too many eggs at once – make several smaller omelettes. Don't overcook the omelette – it should be *baveuse*, slightly runny.

Omelette Fines Herbes Sophistication in simplicity. Prepare a mixture of finely chopped herbs from the garden, classically parsley, tarragon, chives and chervil, using about 1 tablespoon per omelette. Add half to the seasoned eggs and the other half during the cooking.

Omelette Molière A lovely version collected by the late Elizabeth David from a little restaurant she frequented in Avignon. Beat 1 tablespoon finely grated Parmesan cheese with 3 eggs. Make omelette and add 1 tablespoon fresh Gruyère cheese cut into tiny dice and 1 tablespoon heavy cream.

Omelette Arnold Bennett A relic of the days when grand hotels created dishes in honor of their celebrated patrons. This elegant omelette was created for the writer Arnold Bennett at the Savoy Hotel in London, some time in the 1920s.

scant cup smoked haddock
1 cup milk
peppercorns, bay leaf, parsley
8 tbsp heavy cream for poaching haddock

Infuse the flavorings in the milk then poach the haddock in it for 10 minutes. Drain, skin and bone the fish. Flake it and mix with cream. Heat through gently in a small pan until cream has thickened a little. Make omelette and fold onto serving dish. Cut a slit along the top and fill center with spoonfuls of creamed haddock.

Egg and Bacon Pie

No, not a translation of *Quiche Lorraine*, but an almost identical English recipe, dating from 1769.

shortcrust pastry made   1 cup heavy cream
with 1¹/₂ cups flour   salt, freshly ground pepper
1 cup sweet cured bacon   and nutmeg
butter   beaten egg to glaze
4 eggs
(**Serves 4**)

Preheat the oven to 400°F. Make pastry by rubbing about two-thirds of the pastry to line a large pie plate. Chill. Sauté bacon in a little butter until just brown. Beat eggs and cream together with the seasoning. Place bacon pieces over base of pie and pour in mixture. Cover with the remaining pastry, sealing edges well. Brush with beaten egg and bake for 45–50 minutes until lightly set.

Soufflé Omelette with Summer Fruits

Sweet omelettes make a great last-minute pudding for unexpected guests. This version is a fluffy or Belgian omelette, made by beating the whites separately. (Try the same technique for the savory Omelette Arnold Bennett, p. 31).

4 egg yolks
2 tbsp sugar
6 egg whites
1/2 cup mixed summer fruits (strawberries,
raspberries, black/redcurrants etc.)
pat of butter
2–3 cups superfine sugar
1/2 cup thick crème fraîche *or whipped heavy cream*
(Serves 4)

Preheat oven to 425°F. Beat yolks with 2 tablespoons of measured sugar until pale. Beat whites until stiff. Fold yolks and whites into each other carefully. Heat butter in a clean 9-inch omelette or frying pan, pour in the mixture and cook over low heat for 3 minutes. Transfer the pan to the oven for a further 3 minutes or until set. Meanwhile in another pan heat fruit and 1/2 cup of measured sugar just until juice runs and it begins to boil at the edges. Lay out a double sheet of wax paper and sprinkle thickly with sugar. Turn the omelette on to the sugared paper, spread with warm fruit and cream. Quickly fold in two and turn again on to a warm dish. Sprinkle with sugar and serve at once. For a professional finish, dredge with icing sugar and mark a lattice across the top with red hot skewers.

Soufflé Rothschild

To show how the humble egg can rise to the occasion even in the most exclusive company, here is a sweet soufflé created at Maxim's in Paris and name in honor of the famous banking family. There's a clue in the ingredients which include Danziger Goldwasser, a liqueur that contains suspended particles of gold. Don't worry if your local supermarket has run out of the stuff – Kirsch, Cointreau, or rum make excellent substitutes, but don't forget the classic garnish of strawberries. An extra egg white adds lightness to the soufflé.

¹/₂ cup finely diced candied fruit
3 egg yolks and 4 egg whites
6 level tbsp all-purpose flour
4 tbsp liqueur or rum
scant ¹/₂ cup superfine sugar
1 cup milk

confectioner's sugar
fresh strawberries for garnish
For soufflé dish
butter
pinch salt
extra superfine sugar

(Serves 4)

Soak the fruit in the liqueur of your choice for at least 30 minutes or overnight.

To make confectioner's custard base, whisk together the sugar and egg yolks until mixture is white and thick. Mix in flour and hot milk. Pour into a saucepan, bring to the boil, stirring constantly and cook 1–2 minutes. Pour the custard into a bowl and add the fruit and the liqueur. Whisk egg whites to stiff peaks with a pinch of salt and fold carefully into the mixture.

Featherlight Sponge Cake

The discovery of the raising power of eggs, and especially the lightening effect of the air enmeshed in beaten whites, came as watershed in baking refinement. This light-as-air cake, a classic of home baking, is often used as a yardstick for judging the best baker in the parish. A dab of jam and cream and a dusting of sugar are all that this cake needs for melt-in-the-mouth perfection. It can be transformed into a jelly roll, a layered gâteau, or a trifle base.

4 medium-size eggs
$^1/_2$ cup superfine sugar
$^1/_2$ cup self-rising flour, sifted
(Serves 4–6)

Preheat oven to 350°F. Grease 2 x 7 inch sponge cake pans and line bases with wax paper. Separate eggs. Beat yolks and sugar until very pale and thick. Thoroughly clean and dry the whisk. Put whites in a clean bowl and beat until they stand in stiff peaks. Fold into yolk and sugar mixture. Lastly, fold in flour very gently. Divide mixture between pans and bake on the middle shelf of the oven for about 25–30 minutes. The sponges are done when firm and spongy in the center and slightly shrunk from the sides of the pan. Sandwich together with jam, cream, fresh fruit, lemon curd, or a combination of these. Finish with a fine dusting of superfine sugar, or place a paper doilly on the cake and sift icing sugar over it, leaving a pretty pattern behind when it is removed.

Lemon Curd

For the farmer's wife, the contents of her egg basket once provided important pin money though because a strict Lenten fast forbade the eating of eggs until the Easter celebrations, she might find herself with a sudden glut. Thus with a surfeit of eggs lie the probable origins of this peculiarly English preserve. Often eaten on bread and butter or used to fill tartlets, it makes a lovely filling for a sponge cake or for meringues. For a different citrus flavor, use oranges or limes, or try adding a teaspoon of ground ginger and a little crystallized ginger to the mixture before cooking.

2 large washed lemons
4 large eggs
scant cup lump sugar
1/2 cup unsalted butter
(makes approx. 1 lb)

Rub lump sugar on peel of lemon or finely grate zest and mix with sugar. Whisk squeezed juice with eggs, then pour over sugar mixture. Add diced butter, place over pan of barely-simmering water and stir frequently until thickened, about 15–20 minutes. Cool, pot, and cover.

Lemon Curd and Almond Tart

For this delicious tart, line a pie dish with sweet pastry, fill with a layer of lemon curd and top as follows: Cream 6 level tablespoons butter with 6 tablespoons firmly-packed superfine sugar, beat in 1 egg, fold in 1 tablespoon ground almonds and 1 cup self-raising flour with grated rind and juice of one lemon. Spread over curd. Strew generously with split almonds. Bake at 400°F for 15 minutes, then at 300°F for 25–30 minutes.

Snow Eggs

Known also as "Floating Islands," this delicate and attractive dish is a showpiece for the differing properties of yolk and white. Meringue "eggs" are poached in milk that is then used with the yolks to make a custard sauce which, incidentally, the French are pleased to call *crème anglaise*.

Custard: 6 tbsp sugar
2 cups milk 2 tbsp water
1 vanilla bean, split **Meringues:**
(or good vanilla extract) 4 egg whites
4 large egg yolks pinch salt
1/2 cup superfine sugar 1 1/2 tbsp superfine sugar
caramel (optional) toasted almonds (optional)
(Serves 4)

Heat milk with vanilla bean to just below boiling point with vanilla bean and leave to infuse for 20 minutes, or heat milk with extract. Whisk whites to stiff peaks with salt, then fold in superfine sugar. Using a tablespoon, drop batches of meringue mixture into simmering milk, turning gently for a few minutes so that they cook all over. Drain on to a cloth. Measure milk and top up if necessary. Beat yolks into sugar until pale and thick and gradually whisk in the warm milk. Return to clean saucepan and cook gently until mixture coats back of wooden spoon. Strain and stir while cooling. Pour custard into dish wide enough to take the meringues and float the "islands" on top.

To make caramel, place sugar and water in saucepan and boil steadily until a golden caramel is formed. Trickle over meringues and finish, if liked, with toasted almonds.

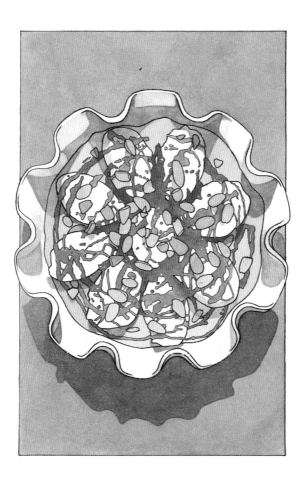

Burnt Cream

Seventeenth century custards were often baked in pastry "coffins" or *croustades* and eaten from them in the absence of individual plates or pots. The charm of this dish, associated historically with Trinity College, Cambridge, is to break through the layer of scorched sugar to get to the custard beneath, barely sweet and subtly flavored. Fresh raspberries or passion fruit make a lovely accompaniment.

2-inch cinnamon sticks
thinly pared peel of 1 lemon
2$^1/_2$ cups heavy cream
6 egg yolks
2 tbsp superfine sugar
demerara or granulated sugar
(Serves 4)

Preheat oven to 325°F . Add cinnamon and lemon to cream in a sturdy saucepan or top of double boiler and heat to just below boiling point. Remove from heat. Beat yolks and sugar until pale and frothy. Gradually stir in the cream. Transfer mixture to top of double boiler or place bowl over barely simmering water and stir lightly until custard just coats the back of a wooden spoon. Strain into shallow ovenproof dish and bake for about 17 minutes or until skin has formed. Remove before it colors, taking care to keep the skin intact. Refrigerate overnight. To finish, heat broiler to maximum, sprinkle custard with sugar evenly all over, to a depth of $^1/_8$ inch. Place under broiler until sugar caramelizes, about 1–2 minutes. Chill thoroughly.

Classic Vanilla Ice Cream

Sunday afternoon in my home town in Ireland meant a trip to Yanarelli's for a big "slider" – real Italian ice cream, churned from a custard base of eggs, milk and sugar, sandwiched between two sweet wafers. Richer versions use only cream, but to me the milk gives an icy lightness that is more refreshing. A *sorbetière* will do the essential job of breaking down the ice crystals as they form, but ice cream was invented long before mechanized churns!

6 egg yolks
scant $\frac{1}{2}$ cup of superfine sugar
1–2 vanilla beans (good vanilla
extract may be substituted)
2 cups milk or half milk, half heavy cream
(Serves 4)

For the custard: Cream yolks and sugar until pale. Combine milk and chopped vanilla beans or extract in a heavy saucepan, bring to boil and simmer for about 5 minutes, or heat milk and extract. Cool for a minute, then pour milk onto eggs and sugar, whisking continuously. Return the saucepan to a medium heat and stir until custard coats the back of a wooden spoon. Strain, cover, and refrigerate until cold.

Churn in an ice cream maker, or stir freeze as follows: Place in container and fast freeze for about 45 minutes until ice forms around edges. Transfer into bowl and stir until smooth. Return to freezer and repeat process once more.

Raspberry Dacquoise

Egg whites that have been frozen will still make excellent meringues. (A good tip is to freeze them individually in ice cube trays.) It is well worth saving up spare whites for this confection. Named after the French town of Dax, it is one of several classic meringue gâteaux made with almonds or hazelnuts.

1¼ cups whole blanched almonds
7 egg whites
1¾ cups superfine sugar
large pinch cream of tartar
2½ cups heavy cream
confectioners' sugar
1½ lb raspberries (fresh or frozen)
superfine sugar
(Serves 4–6)

Grind the almonds coarsely. Whisk egg whites until stiff. Add 1 tablespoon of measured sugar and whisk for a further 2–3 minutes. Fold in rest of sugar with almonds and cream of tartar. Pipe mixture into three separate circles on baking sheets lined with wax paper. Bake at 225°F for 1–1½ hours until dry. Leave to cool. Whip the cream and sweeten to taste with sugar. Sandwich layers, using ⅔ of the raspberries and cream, keeping the remainder to decorate the top. Lastly, dust with confectioners' sugar.

Black Forest Roulade

Here, a light, flour-less chocolate soufflé mixture is baked and then rolled round a filling of black cherries and kirsch-flavored cream. Don't worry if it cracks a little as you roll – that's characteristic and a final dusting of confectioners' sugar will make it look all too enticing.

5 eggs, separated
³/₄ cup superfine sugar
6 squares good quality unsweetened chocolate,
melted to a cream with 2–3 tbsp water
For the filling:
1 lb Morello cherries, canned or bottled
3 tbsp kirsch
1¹/₄ cups heavy cream
(Serves 4–6)

Preheat oven to 350°F. Whisk the egg whites until stiff. In a separate bowl, whisk the egg yolks and sugar until thick and very pale in color. Add the melted chocolate then fold in the whisked egg whites. Spread evenly in a jelly roll pan lined with wax paper. Bake for 15–20 minutes. Cover with a layer of damp kitchen towel. Wrap in plastic wrap and leave overnight. Carefully turn out on to wax paper well dusted with icing sugar and peel off baking paper.

Drain cherries. Moisten *roulade* with a few drops of kirsch and add the rest to whipped cream. Spread cream on *roulade*, add cherries and roll up gently. Dust with confectioners' sugar.

Zabaglione

For this Italian classic and its French cousin, the *sabayon*, egg yolks and Marsala or white wine are whipped up with sugar to produce a yellow velvety foam, eaten at blood heat. A glamorous alternative to cream with fresh fruit and you can also transform it into a wonderful ice cream.

4 egg yolks
4 –6 tbsp superfine sugar
³/₄ cup of Marsala or sweet white wine
(Serves 4)

Whisk yolks and sugar in a bowl until pale and creamy. Gradually whisk in the Marsala or wine. Place a pan of hot water over a gentle heat, set the bowl over it and continue to whisk until mixture thickens and greatly increases in volume. Be patient – it may take 10–15 minutes. Pour into warmed wine glasses and serve.

Spuma di Zabaglione: Simply cool the *zabaglione*, add 1¼ cups whipped cream and freeze. Include little nuggets of dark chocolate if liked.

Pêches au Sabayon: Peel fresh peaches and sandwich halves together with almond paste. Place in a shallow dish, dust thickly with confectioners' sugar and bake for 15 minutes at 325°F. Meanwhile, make a *sabayon* version using white wine. Set peaches in individual glasses, pour over *sabayon* and, for a special occasion, finish with a veil of spun sugar.

Iced Malibu Mousse

The mousse was originally devised as a light pudding, but a fashion later developed for serving it softly frozen. The skill in making a mousse lies in achieving just the right consistency and balance of ingredients. Try this one and enjoy the exotic flavors of a tropical paradise.

3 egg yolks
2 tbsp cold water
¼ cup water with 2 tbsp superfine sugar
and ¼ vanilla bean, split lengthways
1 tbsp each of toasted coconut and grated chocolate
generous cup whipping cream
¼ cup thin custard (see p. 44)
flavored with 1–2 tbsp rum
slices of pineapple and mango to garnish
(Serves 4)

In an electric blender on high speed, beat the egg yolks with 2 tablespoons water for 5 minutes until greatly increased in volume. Meanwhile in a medium saucepan, boil ¼ cup water with the coconut milk, sugar and vanilla for 2 minutes. Remove the vanilla bean, set the blender on low speed and gradually pour the boiling syrup onto the egg yolk mixture. Increase to high speed and continue blending until almost cold. Add the coconut liqueur. Meanwhile beat the cream to a light peak, then fold in the cooled egg yolk mixture. Spoon into 4 lightly-oiled 3-inch ramekin dishes and smooth over the surfaces. Place in the freezer for 5–8 hours to set. Remove to refrigerator 1 hour before needed. Turn out *mousses*. Scatter with toasted coconut, spoon round custard sauce, and garnish with slices of pineapple and mango.

P.S. – Don't Forget the Shell

According to many mythologies, the world was hatched from a giant egg and the ancient custom of decorating eggs, whether it be the intricately etched eggs of the Ukraine, the red eggs of Cyprus, or the bejewelled creations of Fabergé, relates to their significance as a universal symbol of fertility and renewal. The Christian festival of Easter takes its name from the Saxon fertility goddess Eostre on whose feast day eggs were exchanged in celebration of the end of winter. Here, in the spirit of those ancient traditions, is a hair-raising idea for you to try.

Egg Heads

> *brown eggs*
> *paints, etc., to decorate*
> *cotton wool*
> *pkt of cress seeds*

Hard boil eggs and, when cool, cut off tops with a fine serrated knife. Remove contents, scraping out carefully. Gently draw faces on shells using felt tip pens and/or paints. Clowns are always a favorite, or you can make an Indian brave with painted face, fixing on a colored headband with a feather tucked into it. If you have the talent, have a go at a caricature of someone you know. Fill shells with cotton wool, sprinkle cress seed thickly on top and moisten. Cover with polythene until seeds germinate (about 3 days) then leave uncovered on a windowsill out of direct sunlight. Moisten daily and the "hair" will take about 10–14 days to grow to its full glory.

Index

Aïoli 11
Avgolémono 20

Black Forest Roulade 52
Burnt Cream 47

Classic Vanilla Ice Cream 48

Egg and Bacon Pie 35
Egg Heads 59
Eggs Benedict 7
Eggs Mimosa 16
Eggs en Cocotte with Lettuce
    and Bacon 23
Eggs in Madeira Jelly 8

Featherlight Sponge Cake 40

Green Vegetable Tart 28

Iced Malibu Mousse 56

Lemon Curd 43
Lemon Curd and Almond
    Tart 43

Marbled Tea Eggs 12
Millionaire's Eggs 4
Mother's Day Brunch 4

Oeufs à la Tripe 24
Omelette 35
Omelette Arnold Bennett 35
Omelette Fines Herbes 32
Omelette Molière 32

Pêches au Sabayon 55
Pickled Eggs 12
Pipérade 27
Poached Eggs Florentine 15

Quails' Eggs in Poppadom
    Nests with a Curry
    Sabayon 19

Raspberry Dacquoise 51

Scrambling Graciously 4
Seafood Pancakes 31
Skordaliá 12
Smoked Salmon Parcels 4
Snow Eggs 44
Soufflé Omelette with Summer
    Fruits 36
Soufflé Rothschild 39
Spuma di Zabaglione 55

Tapénade 11

Zabaglione 55